NATIONAL GEOGRAPHIC

School Publishing

Soaring
with Science

PIONEER EDITION

By Susan Halko

CONTENTS

2 Soaring with Science

8 Laws at Play

12 Concept Check

Soaring

Lindsey Van waits. She's at the top of the hill. Now the light turns green. Go! She pushes off the bar. She starts down the hill. She's gaining speed. Here comes the jump. What a flight! Her skis are in a perfect V-shape. She is catching air! She glides down. Nice landing. She skis to a stop. What a great jump!

The laws of motion happen when Lindsey jumps. How? What do they have to do with ski jumping? A lot.

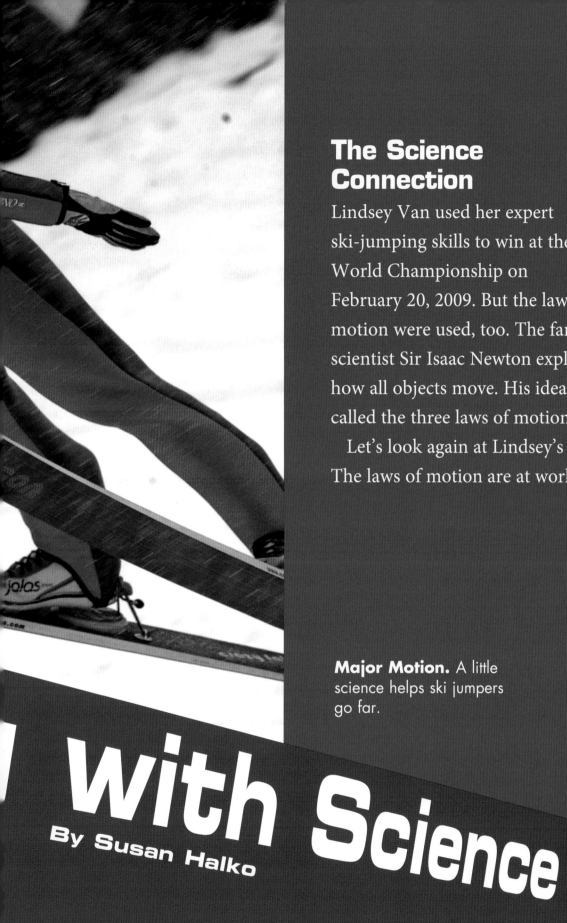

The Science Connection

Lindsey Van used her expert ski-jumping skills to win at the World Championship on February 20, 2009. But the laws of motion were used, too. The famous scientist Sir Isaac Newton explained how all objects move. His ideas are called the three laws of motion.

Let's look again at Lindsey's jump. The laws of motion are at work.

Major Motion. A little science helps ski jumpers go far.

with Science

By Susan Halko

Steps of a Ski Jump

1. In-run   **2.** Take off   **3.** Flight

Forces at Work

Newton's first law says that to move an object at rest, a **force** must get it going. Lindsey pushes off the bar. That force gets her going.

She needs to go fast. As fast as possible! The force of gravity helps. It pulls her down the hill. So she moves faster.

But other forces work against her. Friction happens when her skis rub against the snow. It slows her down. For less friction, Lindsey puts wax on her skis. Her skis slide faster.

Air slows her down, too. Lindsey rushes through the air as she moves. She has to push this air out of the way.

So Lindsey crouches down. This makes her smaller. Now the air flows around her. And Lindsey doesn't have to push against as much air.

More Force = More Speed

Newton's second law says that mass affects how an object speeds up. A smaller person makes a smaller force. That means less speed. So Lindsey's mass affects how fast she can ski.

4. Landing

The Crucial Leap

The in-run takes only a few seconds. Next is the hardest part of the jump. It's the take off. Lindsey jumps up. She jumps out. But it must be just right. Her position and timing must be perfect.

Newton's Three Laws of Motion

Newton told how all objects move. His laws of motion tell about the forces that happen during a ski jump.

First Law of Motion: A moving object keeps moving at the same speed and in the same direction unless a force acts on it. A resting object will stay at rest unless a force acts on it.

Second Law of Motion: The power of the force and an object's mass affect how the object accelerates.

Third Law of Motion: For every action, there is an equal and opposite reaction.

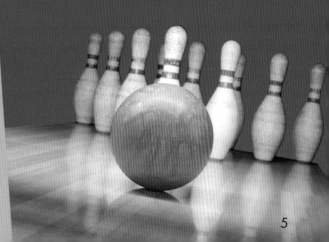

Sweet Victory. Lindsey celebrates! She won the 2009 World Championships!

Need a Lift?

Lindsey gets everything just right. She "catches the air!" This means she is getting **lift**. Lift helps things stay in the air.

Newton's third law of motion tells how lift works. It says for every action, there is an equal and opposite reaction.

A bird flying is a good example of lift. The bird pushes down its wings. So the air pushes the bird up.

As Lindsey soars through the air, her body and skis push air down. That's the action. In turn, the air pushes Lindsey up. That's the reaction.

Lindsey's V-shape position helps her push more air down. In reaction, more air pushes her up. This gives her more lift.

A Happy Landing

Gravity pulls Lindsey back down to Earth. Lindsey lands.

This is another example of Newton's first law of motion. Gravity keeps her from soaring forever.

Lindsey knows she jumped far. In fact, she jumped 97.5 meters (about 320 feet). That's longer than the length of a football field!

As she lands, the edges of Lindsey's skis rub against snow. This **friction** slows Lindsey down. That's okay. She's ready to stop. It's time to celebrate!

Olympic Dreams

Lindsey Van began ski jumping when she was 7. She has long dreamed of winning an Olympic gold medal.

But women ski jumpers were not allowed in the Winter Olympics.

In 2009, the International Olympic Committee still said no. Women's ski jumping still could not be a part of the Winter Olympics. They said there weren't enough skilled women jumpers.

But Lindsey Van and others didn't agree. They knew of 80 women ski jumpers from 14 countries.

They felt that it was not fair. After all, men and women use exactly the same technique during a ski jump.

The only difference is the jumpers' speed. Women need to gain a bit more speed to jump the same distances as men.

Dream Come True

Then in April 2011, the Committee finally accepted women's ski jumping! The 2014 Winter Olympics in Sochi, Russia, will be the first time it is included in the Olympic program.

Wordwise

force: a push or pull

friction: a force that slows down the motion of an object that is touching something else as it moves

lift: a force that helps objects stay in the air

Laws at Play

You don't have to be a top athlete to understand the laws of motion.

Motion is everywhere. Forces are acting on you all the time. Right now, gravity is keeping you on the ground!

You can see the laws of motion anywhere.

Think of a playground. Running around and the merry-go-round show the laws of motion.

Stop Fast

Or think of the swings. A girl swings. She goes higher and higher. She jumps off. She hits the ground. But she doesn't stop. She falls forward.

Another girl is running. She tries to stop fast. But she doesn't stop right away. She moves forward a little.

That's Newton's first law in action! It says that a moving object tends to keep moving unless a force acts on it.

An object at rest stays at rest unless a force acts on it.

The more mass an object has, the harder it is for it to speed up.

Push Me, Please!

Newton's first law also says that an object at rest stays at rest unless a force acts on it.

A child sits in a swing. She is waiting. She wants someone to push her. She's not going anywhere until someone gives her a push.

Faster, Higher!

Finally, the child's mother pushes her gently. She wants to go higher! So her mother uses more force. She gives a bigger push. She's swinging faster! She's swinging higher!

That's Newton's second law in action. It says that a greater force makes an object speed up more.

Heads Up

Sometimes you can't see the forces acting on an object.

Imagine that you're playing catch. The ball goes way over your head.

Newton's first law says that a moving object keeps moving unless a force acts on it. So does the ball keep going? Does it go way up into the sky?

This girl moves forward by pushing back with her foot.

No. Gravity pulls it back down to Earth. When it lands, it rolls on the ground. Do you have to chase it forever? No. Friction slows it down. Then it stops.

Push Back, Go Forward

Newton's third law states that for every action, there is an equal and opposite reaction.

Sometimes you can see this law in action. Think of kids riding their scooters. To move forward, they push one foot back.

Most of the time, you can't see the third law in action. But it's happening.

Think about jumping. As you jump, your foot pushes against the ground. In turn, the ground pushes back.

Everyday Science

Forces are always acting on you. The next time you go to the playground, think like a scientist. Try to see the laws of motion in action.

Laws of Motion

Find out what you learned about forces and the laws of motion.

1 What forces slow Lindsey down as she skis down the hill?

2 What force pulls objects down to Earth?

3 Which force helps Lindsey stay in the air after she jumps?

4 Which of Newton's laws explains why ski jumpers can't stay in the air forever?

5 What law of motion is in use when you give someone a big push on a swing?